Made in the USA
Coppell, TX
14 May 2022

77775656R10063